Charles J Gillis

A Summer Vacation in Iceland, Norway, Sweden and Russia

Charles J Gillis

A Summer Vacation in Iceland, Norway, Sweden and Russia

ISBN/EAN: 9783337298722

Printed in Europe, USA, Canada, Australia, Japan

Cover: Foto ©Andreas Hilbeck / pixelio.de

More available books at **www.hansebooks.com**

A SUMMER VACATION

IN

ICELAND. NORWAY. SWEDEN

AND RUSSIA

BY

CHARLES J. GILLIS

AUTHOR OF "AROUND THE WORLD IN SEVEN MONTHS,"
"ALASKA AND YELLOWSTONE PARK," ETC.

Printed for Private Distribution

.

37 In the Arctic Ocean, 11 P. M.

THE MIDNIGHT SUN.

THE steamship "Ohio," of the American Line, left her dock at Fulton Street, New York, June 26, 1897, having on board ninety excursionists bound for Iceland, Norway, Sweden, Denmark, and Russia. I was glad to join the party, for, with one exception, having already been in every State and Territory of the United States of America, including Alaska; in the most important countries of Asia—Japan, China, Ceylon, and India; in Egypt; and several times in the countries of Europe, with the exception of the ones

5

named above, I desired to complete my knowledge of the globe by taking this trip, particularly as the ship was to go to some places difficult of access and seldom visited by tourists. The steamer proved on examination to be first-class, with all the modern conveniences, and I found myself in possession of a large and very comfortable inside stateroom. She made about 300 miles a day, and was so steady that I often thought she had stopped. The passengers were nearly all Americans—ladies and gentlemen from many parts of the country—notable representatives from Massachusetts, Pennsylvania, New Jersey, Texas, and Mississippi.

In writing an account of this trip I shall endeavor to bear in mind Ruskin's axiom, quoted in one of my previous books of travel, " that the greatest thing a human soul ever does in this world is to see something, and tell what it saw in a plain way."

The countries which we are going to are very old, some of them having histories extending back for more than a thousand years, and the libraries of the world are filled with books describing minutely everything about them. I shall, therefore, try to write what I saw, and not of that which others have seen and written about.

We had a very comfortable passage, and arrived at Southampton July 6th. One day before we landed, one of the young ladies of the party had the misfortune to lose her money belt, containing some sixty dollars in cash and her letter of credit. It had been left in one of the bathrooms, and the theory was that it was found and carried off by a servant who deserted at Southampton.

Early on the voyage I made the acquaintance of Mr. Edward W. Dean, of Rutherford, New Jersey, a retired Boston merchant, and as the ship was detained at Southampton, we went ashore to spend the day and see the sights.

The ship was berthed at the Empress Dock, one of the best

in the world, and the cars of the Southwestern Railway run on to it, so that passengers and freight can be transferred directly from them to the ships.

We wandered about the streets and parks, and found everything clean and orderly. The parks were fine, and adorned with many bronze statues of famous Englishmen, and the grass, trees, and flowers were kept in the best condition. It is a large city, with miles of stores filled with beautiful goods. I bought a soft black hat for four-and-six-pence, and found it a great comfort during the cruise. We had an excellent dinner at a restaurant, and later returned to the ship, and at five o'clock we continued the voyage, passing very near the Isle of Wight and obtaining fine views of the splendid residences and grounds for which that beautiful island is famous. The ship passed on through the Strait of Dover and up the coast of England and Scotland to the

ORKNEY ISLANDS,

where she dropped her anchor in the port of Stromness. The town is a small one, and most of the buildings are apparently one or two hundred years old. Some of the passengers who went ashore stated that the arrival of the ship caused considerable excitement among the people, it being far larger than any American vessel which had ever been seen before.

The town-crier was called to his work, and went about the streets, ringing his bell and shouting:

" Hear ye! Hear ye!
The American steamer " Ohio " has come,
With one hundred passengers on board :
All the shopkeepers put your goods front and tidy,
For you have a chance to make a wee bit of money."

7

A young native woman supplemented this by singing:

" But oh ! ye are grand !
  It will be more than a wee bit ;
  Yee left a deal of money ;
  The likes of it was never seen in all Stromness."

The seventy-three islands in this group belong to Scotland, and the people have the distinguishing characteristics of that race, being religious, sober, intelligent, and law-loving. We were told that there was little use for courts and prisons, and that a murder had not been committed on any of the islands for two hundred years.

We spent an hour or two wandering about the narrow streets and looking into the stores. Some of the ladies bought quite freely of the curios of the place and the well-known Shetland shawls which are woven here.

Leaving this port, the ship made a run of 110 miles to the

SHETLAND ISLANDS,

and landed at Lerwick, Sunday morning, finding all the stores closed, as the town was within Scotch jurisdiction. There are a half dozen churches here, and many of the passengers attended services.

Lerwick is a fine town, much like Stromness, but larger, and presenting a handsome appearance. Seen from the deck of the ship were the town hall, custom house, churches, and many fine dwellings.

A run of 249 miles brought us to the

FAROE ISLANDS.

There are twenty-two of them, belonging to Denmark. We landed at Thorshavn, the principal town, and spent about two hours on shore, looking at the stores and ancient streets and houses. The chief business appears to be fishing, and the curing and exportation of the fish,—rather a bad-smelling occupation, as we discovered here and elsewhere.

A further run of 445 miles brought us to

ICELAND,

the capital of which is Reykjavik, reported to have a population of 4,000. We went ashore here, and spent part of the day looking about. There are no wheeled vehicles to be seen, but any one who wishes can mount a shaggy little horse and go into the country. Some of the party went two miles out of town to see some small hot springs, the water of which was used by the washerwomen of the town; but as I had seen many hot springs in Japan and in the Yellowstone Park, I did not care to endure the manifest discomfort of riding one of the ugly little beasts which were offered to me. A governor, sent from Denmark, resides here, and they have a parliament and senate house, a cathedral, and a hospital,—all of which are very creditable to the country.

We saw a handsome monument, erected to the memory of the great sculptor Thorwaldsen, who was born here, and whose great works can be seen in most of the museums in Europe.

The houses are small, the streets dirty, and the country

9

rough, stony, and very uninviting. Some grass and vegetables were trying to grow, but they had a hard time of it. There was not much snow or ice to be seen, but I consider it the most forlorn country for human beings to live in which I ever saw. The wonder is that the people do not all join some thousands of their fellow countrymen who have a settlement near Winnipeg, Manitoba, where the climate is cold enough in the winter, but fine in summer, and where they can raise wheat and other grains to great advantage. Two years ago I saw several hundreds of people from this settlement who were on an excursion to Winnipeg. They were well clothed, healthy, and nice looking, and I was told that they are very successful farmers.

We stopped two days in Iceland and then started for the North Cape, 1,160 miles off, in a northeasterly direction. Captain Boggs changed the itinerary somewhat, and went entirely around the island. We were only 900 miles from the North Pole, and might have reached it in three days; but as it was reported that we should encounter much ice, we did not move in that direction. The weather continued fine, and the voyage across the Arctic Ocean was very comfortable. I expected to see icebergs and large masses of floating ice in these waters, but I did not. One of the ladies, however, was more fortunate than I, and wrote : " In the afternoon of July 16th I saw a picturesque product of nature's machinery—a large ice-

BOAT LANDING AT THE NORTH CAPE.

10

floe. The sun had separated the iceberg into floating groups of frozen statuary, endless in variety, attractive in form, graceful and dignified in motion; all was aqua-marine, until one short gleam of the sun turned them, for an instant, into jewel caskets, dazzling our eyes with rainbow radiance. This dazzling being a foe to our safety, our good captain changed our course and gave the ice the right of way."

We were in latitude 67° 56' north, and longitude 8° 22' west, and this is a good place in which to see the midnight sun. Heretofore the evenings had been cloudy, and we could not see the sun set; but on the sixteenth of July the weather promised to be clear, and every one was on deck to enjoy the extraordinary sight, which many thousand people go hundreds of miles every summer to see. In this locality the sun does not go below the horizon at this season, but at twelve o'clock begins to rise again. At half-past eleven all hands were eagerly watching the great red luminary—which looked three times as large as usual —until, at a quarter of twelve, it commenced to enter a low bank of clouds resting on the water, and then we were treated to a magnificent sight. To the north and the south the reflection of the sun was cast upon the clouds, forming what appeared to be a vast sea of molten gold. In a short time all this passed; the sun went down behind the clouds, to

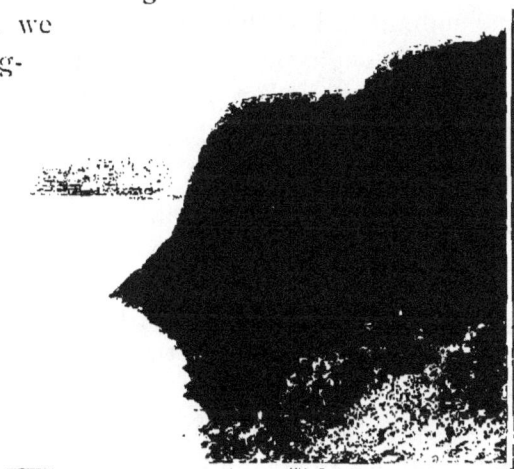

NORTH CAPE FROM THE FOOT-PATH.

II

rise again in ten minutes; but the clouds prevented us from seeing it a second time that night.

At eleven o'clock on the night of July 20th we arrived at

THE NORTH CAPE.

This is described in the guide-books as a dark mass of slate and rock which rises abruptly out of the sea, to a height of 968 feet, and is the most northerly point in Europe. Nearly all the passengers went ashore in the ship's steam launch, and at once commenced the difficult ascent. I was fortunate enough to have for an escort two young ladies from Mauch Chunk, Pa., and we made a brave rush for a third of the way up without stopping. The pathway, running near a small stream of water, was full of rough stones, and the ascent would hardly have been possible but for a rope supported by iron stanchions, which greatly aided our efforts upward. The young ladies proved admirable climbers, and, after two or three halts, we reached the summit in less than thirty minutes, and rested awhile there. It was a tough pull, worse than going up to the top of the Great Pyramid in Egypt, which I did, some years ago, in seventeen minutes; but there I had five Arabs to help me—two to pull, one to push, one to carry water, and one to look on. We then passed on, over a rough field covered with small stones, to the extreme point, and looked out upon the Arctic Ocean. Our watches marked the hour of midnight; but it was foggy, and though light enough to read, there was no sun to be seen.

The photographer of the excursion, Mr. Stoddart, of Glens Falls, N. Y., grouped the party about a round building on the extreme point of the cape, and took our photographs, intending to print them and several hundred others in a large book, with descriptions of the entire trip.

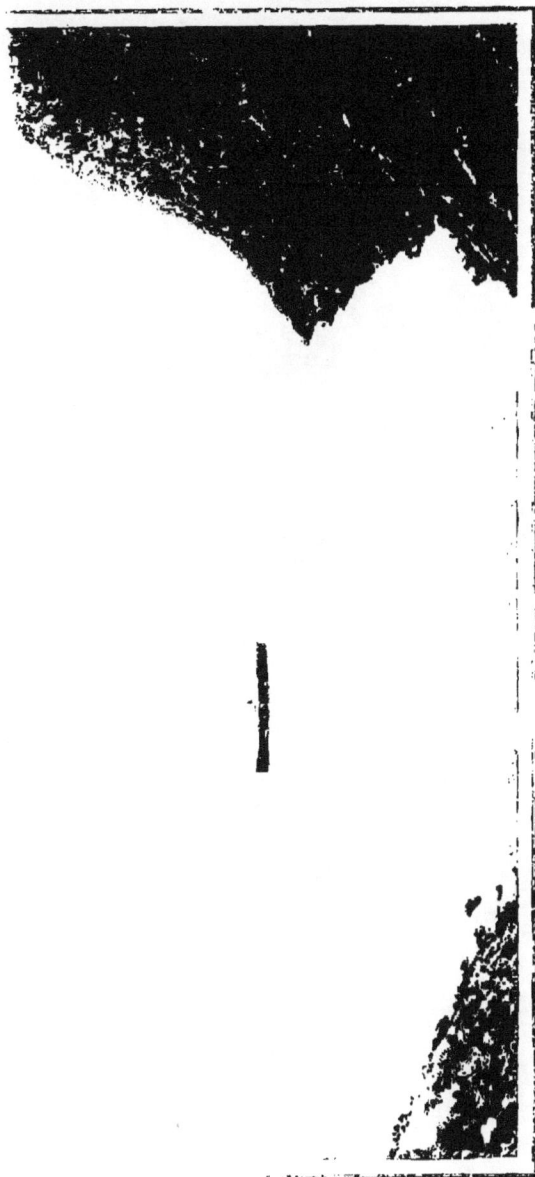

The return down the steep path was almost as rough as the climb up; but we all accomplished it, happily without accident.

Little seven-year-old Marion Dingee, escorted by Captain Boggs, went tripping from stone to stone like a fairy.

We reached the ship at one o'clock A.M., much fatigued, but well pleased that we had done the best we could to see the midnight sun from the top of Cape North.

Next in our course came

HAMMERFEST,

with a population of 2,200, the most northern town in the world, and there we went ashore for two hours. The sun has an erratic way of rising and setting in this region; from May to July, there is sunshine all the time, and from November to January, perpetual darkness; but in this town they get along very well now, having electric lights.

After leaving Hammerfest, Captain Boggs was good enough to invite me on the bridge while we were passing an immense rock on an island called Bird Rock, so named because

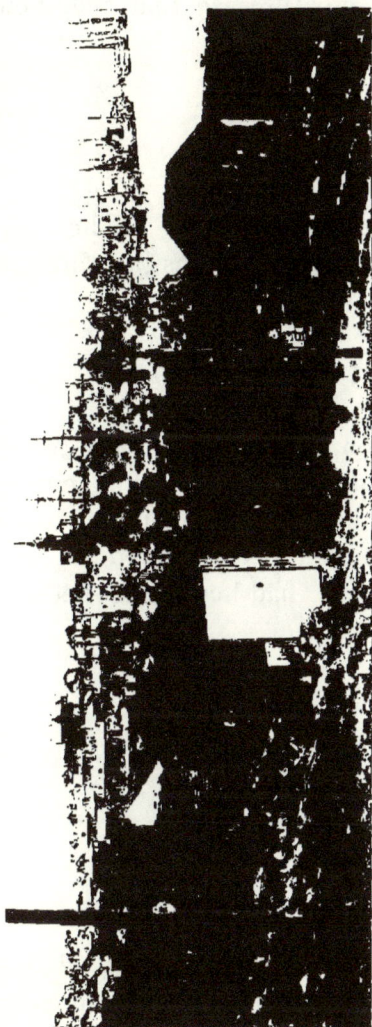

15

HAMMERFEST—TAKEN AT 10 P.M.

it is inhabited by countless thousands of gulls and ducks. As we passed it, steam was let on to a large whistle, which made a tremendous noise, frightening the creatures so that they flew around with loud cries. We then went on to

BOSSEKOP,

a small fishing village of no particular interest. The ship stopped there a few hours and then was off, passing through beautiful scenery to

HARSTAD.

We went ashore and took a long walk through the town, over smooth and excellent roads, as good as you find everywhere in England, France, Germany, and Switzerland. An ancient church was seen; and spruce trees appeared on the mountain sides for the first time, for we had heretofore been in a treeless country.

DIGERMULLEN,

a small place, was passed by on our way to

TRONDHJEM,

an important place, founded eight hundred years ago, and formerly the capital of Norway. Its cathedral is said to be the finest church in Scandinavia. We did not attend the service, although it was Sunday; but we learned from some ladies that the Emperor William of Germany, whose yacht was in these

HAYMAKING, DIGERMULLEN.

waters, was there, with a band of forty pieces of music, and that he himself mounted the pulpit and preached a sermon. The emperor is a frequent visitor to this country, and we were constantly hearing tales of his eccentric actions.

Our next stop was at

MOLDE,

a thriving town of 1,700

PANORAMA OF MOLDE.

inhabitants, from which you get a fine view of a mountain range covered with snow and ice, and also of the fjord. A fjord may be described as an inlet from the sea, running often many miles among the mountains, and deep enough, generally, to float the largest ships. Mr. Dean and I went ashore and took a drive

ON THE ROAD TO ROMSDAL.

through the country in a two-wheeled vehicle, with a boy driver on a seat behind, as on a hansom cab. The roads in this country are excellent, but there are no fences. Our driver must have been asleep, for the horse was not guided, and walked off into a field, upsetting the carriage and throwing us out, but doing no harm, except to alarm

19

our friends at a distance, who saw the accident.

Our next call was at

NAES.

ROAD TO ORMEIM.

We spent the day driving through the famous Romsdal Valley, and for the first time saw the really magnificent scenery of Norway in all its grandeur. We went on the road along the banks of a river, with great mountains on both sides, and in the valley were fine farms, with fields of oats, grass, potatoes, and barley in good condition, and largely attended to by stout and, in many cases, comely women.

At Ormeim, fifteen miles distant, we had an excellent lunch, and, returning by the same route, reached the ship at five o'clock.

It has been well said that " the gorge, or valley, presents a spectacle of grandeur not easily forgotten : the high, perpendicular walls; the bare and rugged mountains, with dark and deep crevices; and the black-striped, abrupt

ON THE ROAD TO ORMEIM.

UPPER LIERFOSSES, EAST FALL.

sides of the hills and rocks gave a peculiarly sombre aspect to the scene." "At Ormeim the river receives the waters of a stream, forming a magnificent cascade, which divides itself into three branches, each one tumbling down the sides of the hills in foaming billows." Some of the waterfalls which we saw plunged down 2,000 feet. These falls were numerous. I never saw so many near together, except in Japan.

Leaving Naes, a run of 258 miles took the steamer to

MUNDAL,

where we arrived at 11 A.M., having passed through some of the most magnificent scenery in the world. Once, on looking back, it seemed to me as if a mighty gate had closed us in, and there was no way of getting out, surrounded, as we were, with snow-capped mountains five thousand feet or more high; but an opening soon appeared, and we passed on to see other views equally fine. We went ashore here and took a drive on the perfect roads over the mountains, and looked upon scenery quite as grand as any in the Alps in Switzerland.

The glaciers seen from here are a great attraction. They appear to be three or four miles off, and are much smaller than those in Switzerland, and not to be compared with those in Alaska—the Muir, for instance, being about two miles wide, two or three hundred feet high, and several hundred miles long; while from it great masses of ice, often as large as a church, constantly fall into the water.

Our next call was at

BALHOLMEN,

where we arrived on the evening of the 29th, and went ashore the next morning. Magnificent Alpine scenery, great mountains covered with snow and ice, were to be seen everywhere. The steamer sailed to the grand Fjord Aurland. The depth of the sea at the entrance is said to be 3,000 feet.

Then we went on through still more magnificent scenery, if possible, to

GUDVANGEN,

a small hamlet situated among blocks of stone torn from the mountain side. We went ashore in the morning, and commenced a never-to-be-forgotten trip over the mountains to Bergen, where we were to rejoin the steamer. Mr. Dean and I tried to secure a four-wheeled vehicle, but they were all engaged, and we were obliged to take the dangerous-looking two-wheeled affair with the driver seated behind. Our previous experience, however, caused us to reject a boy driver, and we got a careful-looking fellow who owned the team, and so would presumably be careful of that, if he were not of his passengers. The road was an excellent one, built with great engineering skill, up the mountains, and following for some distance the banks of a river. Everywhere we looked upon superb scenery, the like of which is not often seen.

While passing for some miles along the banks of a lake, we saw a stone monument erected to mark the spot where Mr. and Mrs. Youmans, of New York, were drowned on the Fourth of July, 1896. Their horse was frightened or ugly, and backed off into the water. We stopped for a few minutes to read the inscription on the monument, and then the driver started the horse, which commenced backing toward the lake in a most alarming manner; but Mr. Dean took hold of the reins and kept him from doing so. We then drove on through more splendid scenery to

STALHEIM.

After lunch here, we continued the journey, soon going down a steep mountain road on the banks of a large river, at terrific speed, arriving at 5 P.M. at

VOSSEVAVEN.

The hotel is situated half-way up a high mountain, not readily accessible for carriages, and most of us walked up an exceed-

THE WEST HARBOR AND FORTRESS, BERGEN.

ingly steep, zigzag path a mile long; a very fatiguing climb— almost as much so as the one up on the North Cape.

The view from the hotel, of the rushing and foaming river

27

below, the snow-clad mountains above and around, in fact the entire landscape, was one of exceeding beauty. The hotel at which we spent the night was an excellent one in every way.

In the morning we took the steam cars for

BERGEN,

arriving there about noon, and going immediately on board the ship. Bergen is an important seaport city of 55,000 inhabit-

ROAD, LAKE, AND BUARKBRAE GLACIER.

ants, and is picturesquely situated, with a background of high hills. We took a long drive into the country, and visited an encampment of Laps, who made rather a sorry show with their poor little reindeer. The ship went along in the evening and stopped next at

GUDVANGEN HARBOR.

ODDE.

The following morning we took a drive along the banks of a river and a lake for sixteen miles through continued magnificent scenery — a combination not often seen of river, lake, and snow-capped mountains.

We happened to arrive at Mirror Lake just in time to see the reflection of the mountains on its surface, and it was a sight of exceeding beauty. I think the view of Odde and the fjord below, as seen from the mountains, one of the

most beautiful in all the world. We saw many water-falls, one of which, the Skiaeggedalfoss, 1,600 feet high, is said to be the finest in Norway. After dining at a hotel, we went aboard the ship and left the next morning for

STAVANGER,

sailed up a fine fjord, and again saw more splendid scenery—a

great glacier and snow-covered mountains. The fjord here is said to be one of the grandest in Norway, being enclosed by cliffs 3,300 feet high.

Here we left the beautiful Norwegian scenery. Tourists who have plenty of leisure might spend a week to great advantage in any of the places where we spent only a day or two. The hotels are excellent and cheap, and the people models of intelligence, honesty, sobriety, and good looks—particularly the young women. We saw no tramps, beggars, drunkards, or very poor people.

A run of 356 miles brought us to

COPENHAGEN, DENMARK,

which has a population of 376,000. Mr. Dean and I stayed at the Hotel Metropole, and for two days went about the city, and

VIEW FROM STALHEIM HOTEL.

found it to be one of the finest in Europe. Parks, palaces. churches, and streets—all are splendid. We dined and spent an evening at the Tivoli Gardens, a very large and elegant place, where a free concert, which was very fine and largely attended, was given in one of the buildings.

Another run, this time of 438 miles, brought us to

STOCKHOLM, SWEDEN,

where we went ashore, and finding all the rooms engaged at the Grand Hotel, one of the best, we secured excellent ones at the Hotel Swede, which was near, and took our meals at the Grand. We drove and walked about the city for three days, visiting picture galleries and public places, and we all pronounced it to be a splendid city, as fine as the best in any country. The population is about

A NARROW STREET IN THE OLD QUARTER, STOCKHOLM.

200,000, distributed between the mainland and nine islands connected by numerous bridges.

A great exhibition was being held in a beautiful park. This we attended, and spent most of a day looking at the collection of goods and manufactures from all parts of Scandinavia. We also visited a gallery of fine paintings, and we would have liked to stay in the city at least a fortnight, in order to get a really good idea of its many beauties.

The next stop was at

HELSINGFORS,

the capital of Finland, a place not in my geography, and I was much surprised to find a large city, with fine streets, blocks of

RUSSIAN CHURCH, HELSINGFORS.

buildings that would adorn any city, and a senate house; for though Finland is a part of Russia, it has a parliament. Here we saw for the first time the Russian vehicle called a drosky, a low, four-wheeled carriage, having seats for two only, besides the driver in front. Accompanied by my little friend Marion, I drove all about the city and then returned to the ship.

A further sail of 162 miles brought us to the famous fortified town of

CRONSTADT, IN RUSSIA.

We arrived at seven in the morning, and spent the day on the ship, as we were not allowed to land. The custom-house

ODDE AND HARDANGER FJORD.

officers came on board, examined all
our passports, endorsed them, and in
the evening permitted the ship to go
on. The city is a large one, reported
as having 100,000 inhabitants, and, as
seen from the ship, it appeared to be
a fine city, with lofty buildings, an immense church,
and parks, and it was surrounded by great fortifica-
tions. The Emperor Will-
iam's yacht passed us here,
and later we saw that of
Mr. George Gould. We
went along through a canal,

STATUE OF PETER THE GREAT, ST. PETERSBURG.

nine miles long and very wide, toward St. Petersburg. The
canal was crowded with all kinds of craft—steamers, yachts,
sailing vessels, and boats loaded with grain and lumber. Our
big ship was in charge of a Russian pilot, and he skillfully
avoided collision between her and any other craft until near the
end of the route, when she ran into and sunk a large wooden
canal boat laden with grain, and made great holes in two others.
After this she continued her course, and soon cast anchor at

ST. PETERSBURG,

near the famous St. Nicholas Bridge. The next day we drove
about the city in a drosky. It contains more than a million of
people, and is immense, being six miles long and five miles wide.
The streets are long and very wide, lined with great numbers of
splendid churches, public buildings, stores, and houses; and,
altogether, it is one of the most picturesque and splendid cities

in Europe. I noticed, as we drove along at a rapid pace over the cobble-stone pavements, that the drosky man was constantly crossing himself whenever we passed a church or what is called an " icon "—the picture of a saint in a frame. These images are fastened up at frequent intervals along the streets.

MONUMENT OF NICHOLAS II., ST. PETERSBURG.

We were housed at the Grand Hotel, an excellent one, and there, immediately on our arrival, our passports were examined again, and endorsed. We went through the Hermitage, one of the finest picture galleries in the world, and many other public buildings, filled with costly and elegant things, which it would take a whole guide-book to describe.

I attended service several times at St. Isaac's Cathedral, whose big gilded dome you see from great distances, and in front of which stands the famous statue of Peter the Great. The vast church was filled with at least ten thousand people, standing up, for there are never seats in a Greek church. The people appeared to be mostly of the poorer classes, roughly clothed, but they were very attentive to the service. Every few minutes those around me would kneel down, strike their heads on the marble floor, and then get up and make the sign of the cross. The services appeared to be wholly musical, and such music I never heard. An old, long-bearded bass singer came forward and sung, filling the vast edifice with wonderful melody ; and he was followed with half a dozen others, who sung together very sweetly.

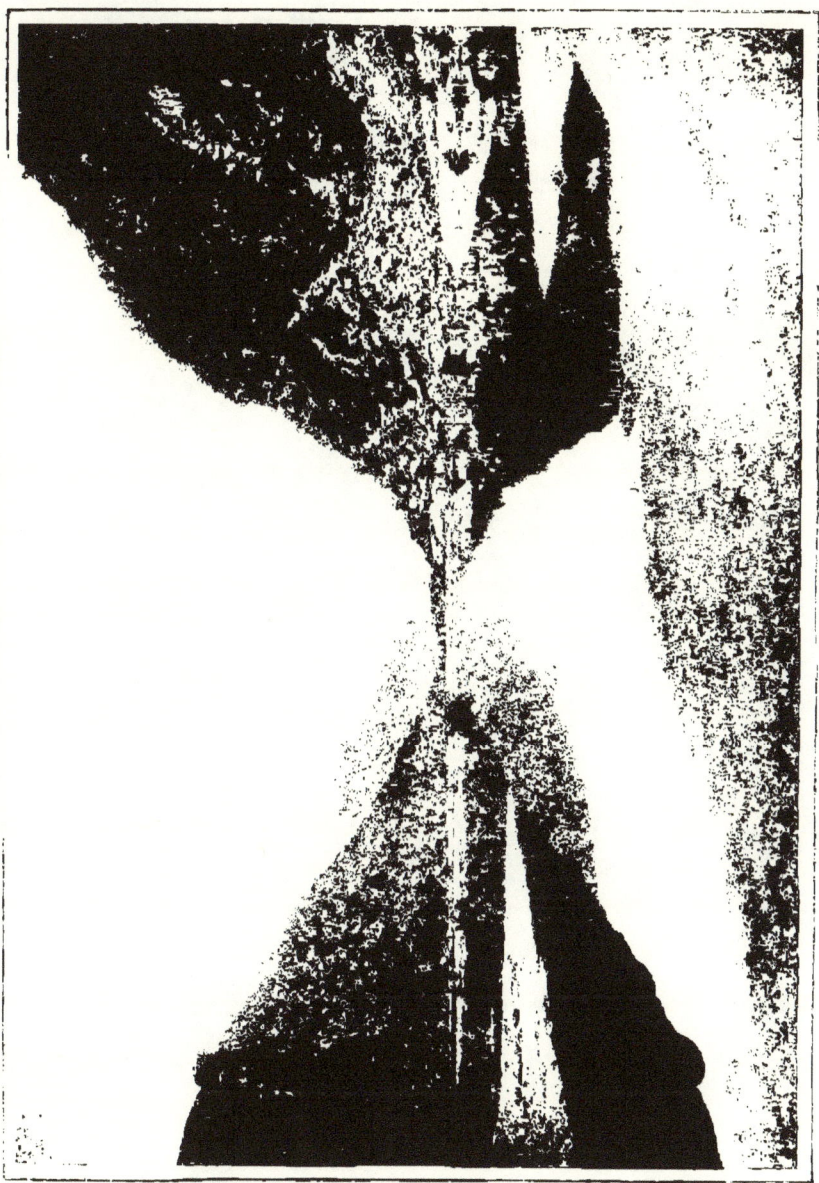

The decorations of this church were marvels of costly extravagance. The paintings of many saints were framed in solid silver adorned with precious stones. I examined with great interest a beautiful model of the church, about three feet long, two wide, and two high, made of solid gold. Peter the Great is much in evidence everywhere; his palaces, the house he built and lived in, the chair he sat in, the desk he used, and a portrait of him, the frame studded with diamonds, are shown.

We left by rail at eight in the evening for

MOSCOW,

403 miles distant. This road was built by Philadelphia contractors, and engineered by Major George W. Whistler, of Boston, whom I remember seeing once when I was a lad. It is well built, and as good a road as I ever was on. The cars are first class, run by an international company, whose headquarters are in Paris. They are of the Mann boudoir pattern. Before getting to bed, and also in the morning, we had a chance to see the country through which we were passing. We did not see any large towns or many farms. The country was perfectly flat. We arrived at Moscow at 11 A.M., and stopped at the Hotel Berlin, an excellent one in every respect. After lunch we took a drosky and were rushed over the rough cobble pavements at a fearful speed to the famous Kremlin, situated on the hills, and enclosed

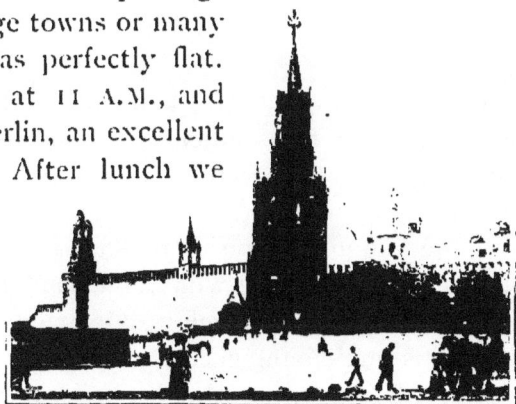

THE HOLY GATE OF THE KREMLIN, MOSCOW.

43

by a wall sixty feet high and two miles long. Here we had a splendid view of the city, with its "marvellous conglomeration of domes and spires—like melons, pumpkins, pears, and strawberries, ornamented with spirals, circles, and zigzags; hung with chains, disks, crescents, and stars; gilded with gold, covered with copper, or painted bright red or green." Murray's handbook devotes forty-eight pages to a description of the churches and buildings and their contents within the Kremlin, and from reading them one can get an idea of the splendor of the edifices and their immensely valuable contents. We went into a beautiful and costly little church where the emperor was lately crowned; we were also escorted to the rooms which Napoleon occupied, in which we saw the bed he slept on and the chairs he used. We could not fail to recall that, in September, 1812, he looked out of the same windows which we were now gazing from, and saw the great fires burning which destroyed the beautiful city. He sent a message suggesting peace to Kutusow, the commander-in-chief of the Russian army, who replied: "There will be no peace as long as there is one foreign soldier on Russian soil. The campaign has just commenced."

We all remember the frightful retreat of the French army from Moscow. One hundred and ten thousand soldiers marched

THE GREAT BELL, MOSCOW.

THE ENGLISH CHURCH, COPENHAGEN.

into Russia, and only 10,000 ever reached the soil of France.

I was much interested in the great bell, the largest in the world, cast in 1733, and weighing 288,000 pounds. There is a fracture in it, caused, as I had always read, by a fall, but this is a fable. It was housed in a tem-

CHURCH OF ST. BASIL, MOSCOW.

porary shed, which was burned, and the water thrown on to put out the fire caused the fracture.

Moscow is a very busy place, being a railroad centre and great manufacturing seat. It is several hundred miles further east than Constanti-

ENTRANCE TO KREMLIN FROM CHINESE TOWN, MOSCOW.

nople, and has trade with both Oriental and Western countries. Several times, when looking at the minarets and fancy buildings, I thought I must be in India or Turkey. I found diamonds and furs much cheaper than with us, but all other things very high priced.

We made the return trip to St. Petersburg by night, arriving there at 11 A.M., and this time we stayed at the Hotel del' Europe, one of the largest and finest in Europe, complete with modern appliances, including steam heat, electric lights, and water in the bedrooms, and a table all that could be desired.

The next day we went on a steamboat about eight miles to

PETERHOF,

and saw what appear to me to be altogether the most magnificent pleasure grounds and fountains in the world. The fountains do not usually play except on holidays or by command, but we were fortunate enough to be there when the President of France was expected, and saw them all in full operation. Some years ago my friend Mrs. Daniel Butterfield was presented to the court, and the empress ordered the fountains played especially for her.

There were a dozen or more large statues of glittering gold, scattered along the walks and among the trees, with great quantities of water flowing over and around them, producing beautiful effects. There were two designs which I had never seen before, except at Chatsworth, England, the seat of the Duke of Devonshire, one being a series of a hundred or more marble steps, down which tumbled a great mass of water; and the other what appeared to be a large natural willow tree, but it turned out to be made of copper, and when the man in charge turned on a cock, water fell from each leaf. We spent several hours in

ST. ISAAC'S CATHEDRAL, ST. PETERSBURG.

walking and driving through the beautiful woods and well cared for parks; went through another glittering and splendid palace; saw another house where Peter the Great once lived; and then took the train for St. Petersburg, arriving there in half an hour.

I think we were fortunate in being at Peterhof at the time of the immense preparations for the reception of the President of France; and we know that two days after we left he met the emperor, they embraced with enthusiasm, and thus cemented friendship between two of the most powerful nations on earth, —France with her glorious history of hundreds of years, on the pages of which stand out the names of her great men, surrounded, as it were, with circles of diamonds, flashing in the midday sun so that all men may see them for ages to come: who cannot recall the names of Voltaire, Napoleon, Murat, Ney, and hundreds of others, and later on those of Guizot, Thiers, Gambetta, and the scientists and scholars who have, since its foundation, made the French Academy famous throughout the world; and Russia, with her enormous possessions extending from sea to sea, her immense population and wealth, appearing now to be entering upon a career which will ultimately place her among the foremost nations of the earth in civilization, as she already is in power. She has nearly completed a railroad from Vladivostock to St. Petersburg, 6,000 miles long, the longest continuous railway in the world, and another running to the Chinese Sea; and everybody knows that railways are the greatest missionaries of modern times. They run around, under, and over great ranges of mountains; span valleys and streams, and penetrate vast forests; to be followed by towns and cities, bringing with them civilization, education, and religious influences. Our visit to Russia may prove to have been at an epoch-making period in the history of civilization and the world.

The next day we went on board the ship and again passed through the canal to

CRONSTADT,

where the custom-house officers examined our passports, endorsed
them, and then permitted us to leave the country, and we went
on into the Gulf of Finland. The passengers were so well
pleased with the cruise on the " Ohio," that one evening they
presented to Captain Boggs, through Dr. J. N. Bishop, of New
York, who made a graceful address, a paper signed by all, thank-
ing him for his politeness, and congratulating him and his officers on the entire success of the trip. I heartily endorse what
Dr. Bishop said, and the contents of the paper presented to
Captain Boggs; and that thanks are also especially due the
chief officer, Mr. E. V. Roberts, for, though constantly engaged
night and day attending to his duties in navigating the ship, he
always found time to be polite in his attentions to the passengers. I also wish to say that the fourth officer, Mr. F. O. Hor-
ton, who generally had command of the steam launch which
carried the passengers to and from the shore hundreds of times, is
to be commended for his constant watchfulness and care, so that
not the slightest accident ever occurred, and the passengers were
always treated by him with courtesy and politeness.

The ship passed on 782 miles to

KIEL,

where my friends Mr. Dean, Mr. and Mrs. Flack, and several
others got off, wishing to go through Germany to Paris. The
steamer went through the Kaiser Wilhelm Canal. This canal is
61½ miles long, 31 feet deep, and 200 feet wide, with only two
locks, one at each end, and I saw only two bridges. It passes
through a level and cultivated country, with many houses and
villages on or near its banks. The United States steamer

52

THE KREMLIN, FROM ACROSS THE RIVER, MOSCOW.

"Charleston" went through the canal when it was dedicated, but no ship from America as large as the "Ohio" had been seen since, and the banks were often lined with men, women, and children, who smiled and cheered as we passed.

We were nine hours going through the canal, and then we found ourselves on the ocean once more. We reached Southampton on the morning of the twenty-fifth of August, after an absence from New York of sixty days, during which time we had had nearly perfect weather. Captain Boggs and everyone else on the ship knew that this was because we had on board a mascot —the little seven-year-old Marion Dingee, who was constantly running up and down stairs and all over the ship, carrying with her light, sunshine, and beauty.

When the passengers stood on the deck of our ship in foreign seas, we were like a man in a great forest, who, when he saw a blaze on the trees, knew that by following the path indicated, it would lead him to a haven of safety; so we, when we looked aloft and saw the Star Spangled Banner floating at mast, knew that all who stood beneath its folds were entitled to life, liberty, protection, and the pursuit of happiness.

As the stately vessel passed through many waters and into many countries, we saw that flag saluted in recognition of the fact that it represented one of the great powers of earth, the United States of America. Let us, therefore, continue to cherish that flag, and in our distant homes see that it floats on festival days, on the hills and in the valleys, on schoolhouse and other public buildings, and, in the language of General Dix, "If any man hauls it down, shoot him on the spot."

At Southampton I left the ship, took the night boat for Havre, and arrived in Paris early the next morning. After four days in Paris, I recrossed the channel by way of New Haven, went to London, stayed there four days more, and then came home in the fast steamer "St. Paul."

Thus ended another summer vacation.

www.ingramcontent.com/pod-product-compliance
Lightning Source LLC
Chambersburg PA
CBHW031800090426
42739CB00008B/1088